James Geraghty

The Present State of Ireland,

and the only means of preserving her to the Empire, considered. : In a

letter to the Marquis Cornwallis.

James Geraghty

The Present State of Ireland,
and the only means of preserving her to the Empire, considered. : In a letter to the Marquis Cornwallis.

ISBN/EAN: 9783337101947

Printed in Europe, USA, Canada, Australia, Japan

Cover: Foto ©Suzi / pixelio.de

More available books at **www.hansebooks.com**

THE

PRESENT

STATE OF IRELAND,

AND

THE ONLY MEANS OF PRESERVING HER

TO

THE EMPIRE,

CONSIDERED.

IN A

Letter to the Marquis Cornwallis.

By JAMES GERAGHTY, Esq:

BARRISTER AT LAW.

Concordiâ res parvæ crefcunt.

LONDON:

PRINTED FOR J. STOCKDALE, PICCADILLY.

1799.

PRESENT STATE,

&c.

MY LORD,

PULCHRUM est bene facere reïpublicæ, etiam bene dicere haud abfurdum est, is the obfervation of the eloquent hiftorian, who has tranfmitted to us the details of that flagitious confpiracy which once menaced the Roman name, and which the vigilance and patriotifm of the chief magiftrate detected and defeated.

Your Excellency may perceive with what application the opinion and authority of the illuftrious Roman can be urged in this addrefs. The arduous fituation in which you have been placed by your appointment to the government of Ireland, may bear fome likenefs to that of the diftinguifhed conful, whom the Roman writer has recorded as the father of his country. In an hour of extraordinary danger and confternation, armed like him with fupreme authority, *ne quid detrimenti refpublica capiat*, you have effected the public fafety ; but without violation of the law, or departure from the duties of humanity. In this your Excellency, without vanity, might claim, and Truth herfelf muft recognife your

B   fuperiority

superiority to the Roman magistrate. The late conspiracy in Ireland, for extent, system, and preparation, has no parallel in the confederacy of Catiline. They may resemble in boldness of design, and flagitiousness of means; but their difference is incalculable, when we compare the two æras which are stained with their enormities, and contrast the darkness of paganism with the light of christianity. The face of human society is considerably varied since the days of Cicero; the arts of life have been since perfected; navigation and commerce have connected and civilized the nations of the earth; a complete interchange of wisdom has every where educated the minds, and softened the manners of men; the principles of government are brought to a just theory; whose great end is the happiness of the people; and a wise and extended policy has arisen in Europe, whose end is the security and independence of separate states, by an equalization of power, which, like the pressure on the parts of a fluid when equal and general, sustains the whole in tranquillity.

The system of morals introduced by christianity, and interwoven in the frame of civilized states, has diffused the purest and most exalted notions of morality. Considering these, and the many important discoveries, and improvements of modern times, the late transactions in Ireland fill us with astonishment, and lead the philosophic observer to deep and serious reflection. From your conduct, my Lord, at all times in the service of your sovereign, and the zeal and promptitude with which you obeyed his late commands in assuming the government of a considerable part of his dominions, in a season the most difficult and trying, when the powers of ordinary men are found inadequate to the great emergencies which arise; and when your Lordship's refusal would have stood justified by your long and important services, and the claims of that period of life, to which you have happily arrived: from these, my Lord, and the experience of superior wisdom in your government;

ment, the Public are induced to hope, that, under your Lordſhip's auſpices, the victory which has been acquired, may be ſecured ; that the enemy may not recover from his defeat ; and that the King's faithful ſubjects in Ireland may not feel a return of calamity. Humbly to ſuggeſt to your Excellency the meaſure eſſential to produce this good, to trace the real object of the rebellion, and aſcertain the real motives of its leaders, is the deſign of this addreſs.

From the relation of the two countries, and the incorporation of their commercial and political inte-reſts, the tranſactions of one cannot be indifferent to the other ; nor can the head of the empire view, without the deepeſt concern, the diſſentions which continually agitate, and the miſchiefs which occaſi-onally deſolate a country, which, under an enligh-tened policy, were capable of the higheſt proſperity.

The firſt and great duty of government which is truly parental, is, ſo to form and diſcipline the pub-lic mind by regulation and inſtitution, that it ſhall not have opportunity to err, or temptation to be vicious ; to exclude the occaſion of crimes, rather than pu-niſh their commiſſion ; that the ſubordination of the ſtate may proceed more from virtue than neceſſity. Every principle of duty which actuates a govern-ment, inculcates this particular obligation, which, as it may apply to Ireland, excluſive of its moral claim, is irreſiſtibly enjoined by the politics of Eng-land ; thoſe politics which have united her at home, and made her formidable abroad. To rivet the parts of the empire in unity of will and law ; to conſoli-date their ſtrength and intereſts ; to multiply the energy, and augment the reſources of Great Britain, muſt be the wiſh of every Engliſhman ; and can Ireland heſitate to ſhare her freedom and her glory, her talents and her induſtry, her wealth and tran-quillity ? In England, the prejudices of the few muſt give way to the policy of the whole ; and, in Ireland, the ſad experience of misfortune muſt counteract the ſuggeſtions of pride ; and inducing the people there

to

to contemplate with ferioufnefs the condition of their country, muft infpire them to embrace with eager-nefs, and tolerate with equanimity, fuch conftituti-onal changes as reafon may demonftrate to be indif-penfible for continuing to them the bleffings of tran-quillity.

That your Excellency is well difpofed to promote this great meafure, is not a matter of doubt. The public eftimate of your character is not more flatter-ing than juft. A few whom faction depraves, or bigotry deludes, may deny you the praife which is due, and load you with invective; but the great majority of the people are fatisfied of the rectitude of your in-tentions, and the wifdom of your meafures. The prefent occafion is not above your talents; you have been long habituated to the duties and difficul-ties of government, and will not, I am perfuaded, reject without confideration, or from want of confi-dence abandon an opportunity for confirming all the good you have done, and rendering the empire effen-tial and permanent fervice. Seldom, to be fure, has Ireland a Viceroy, whofe meafures of govern-ment look beyond the term of his adminiftration: to fecure a majority in Parliament, and tranfact the King's bufinefs, as it is called, without clamour or oppofition, is the whole of their efforts; but it is well known, that your Excellency went to Ireland induced neither by ambition nor emolument—a more comprehenfive and liberal policy therefore has marked, and muft continue to characterize, your adminiftration.

If ever the general circumftances of the empire, or the particular ftate of Ireland, required that her government fhould be committed to extraordinary talents, and more than human firmnefs, it has been during the prefent feafon. An active and perfidious foe has availed himfelf of every opportunity for af-faulting the power and undermining the government of Great Britain, and civil diffenfions have raged in Ireland, which threatened her with more danger than

the

the wiles of the common enemy; at this juncture was your Excellency called to her government, in which your conduct has manifested the great qualities required for the situation. Many of your predecessors in this high office have had their share of sense and understanding; many men of good intentions have filled the illustrious roll; but in general their love of ease and luxury incapacitated them for the labours of government, and enslaved them to the views and artifices of a party, whom they came to command. This has uniformly impeded all scrutiny of injustice, and all reformation of abuse. The administration of the Marquis of Buckingham, however, must be admitted as an honourable exception. This has proved the bane of Ireland. The state chariot, amidst all the changes of its possessor, has rolled the same way without variety or deviation; but time has impaired its strength and multiplied its impediments. The moment for its reparation has arrived, or ruin threatens the chariot and its guide. In your Lordship the Public have found a mind above the attractions of indolence and pleasure, too high to obey what it should command, and too honest to neglect any of its duties. To your Excellency therefore does Ireland look for providence as to her future condition, as well as for ability, temper, and integrity, in regulating her present affairs.

It is surprising how much the internal concerns of Ireland are misrepresented in England, and how little is the information abroad of the real state of that country. From this ignorance has the British Cabinet proceeded blindfold in the management of Ireland; their knowledge of Irish affairs is through the medium of the Viceroy, who reports nothing from his own experience; he is the slave of pleasure, and the agent of his own servants. On his arrival in Ireland he finds an aristocracy holding the keys of Parliament, and in possession of all the great offices of state; an *imparlance* instantly takes place, and the result of this *concord* and agreement is, the Viceroy's

transferring

transferring to the aristocracy all the real and virtual power of government, with the authority of the King's name, in exchange for personal repose, a polite court, and an accommodating Parliament. Hence the statements of successive Governors to the British Cabinet are all of one complexion; not a single ray of light beams on them from any quarter; all is ignorance and darkness. Besides the inertness and inactivity of the Viceroy, other causes may contribute to the want of information, as well as mismanagement of Irish affairs, which it may be useful to examine.

Remotely situated as Ireland is from the fountain of her government, she must in some measure feel the inconvenience of provincial dependency. The common sovereign of both countries can reside in but one; Ireland therefore, as junior and inferior, can enjoy only the reflection of the royal light. She must therefore, from the nature of things, be more subject to abuse, and less likely to be redressed; besides, her distance from the royal ear renders it necessary that her government should be vicarious, which subjects her to further inconvenience. The Sovereign living in the midst of his subjects has an interest in their happiness, and in the peace of his kingdom, at least for the term of his life; the Viceroy bounds all his views within the period of his administration only, which can continue but a few years, and which a thousand causes may terminate prematurely, without reference to impropriety of conduct. The Monarch at his birth derives his duties from nature, and his whole education is how to discharge them; the Viceroy is the steward, whose rectitude is matter of accident, and whose interest contravenes his duty. The character of one is original and parental, affectionate and permanent; of the other, derivative and tutelary, selfish and fleeting. The effects of this difference in character are obvious, and are abundantly confirmed in the history of Ireland. The statute of Henry the Seventh, known by the name of Poyning's Act, which made it necessary

to

to tranfmit into England the feveral bills intended to
be paffed in the Parliament of Ireland previous to
their introduction there, and to exemplify the caufes
and reafons for holding parliament, was enacted for
the fole purpofe of protecting the Englifh colony
from the oppreffion and exaction of the King's reprefentative. This very act, which put the Irifh fettlement under the immediate protection of the Englifh
Government, and fhielded it from the rapacity of
governors, became in fubfequent time, by a ftrange
perverfion, the object of popular odium and the fubject of general diffatisfaction in Ireland : the people
there were taught to view in it an unjuft control in
the Britifh Parliament, proceeding from force and
ufurpation ; though the hiftory of that act, and its
own provifions, demonftrate the parental affection
and benevolence of England for that country. Not-
withftanding the difadvantage attending the exercife
of the royal authority through the medium of a deputy
in Ireland, were there any connection between her
Legiflature and that of England, if the Englifh Parliament had a fuperintending power to examine and
decide on the affairs of Ireland, the inconvenience of
vice-regal government would hardly exift, more particularly if Ireland were a conftituent of the Britifh
Parliament, and had immediate and direct accefs to
its counfels by regular reprefentation. However, at
prefent fhe has an independent and feparate Legiflature, which, however it oppofe vulgar notions, and
give offence to popular prejudice, I fhall not fcruple
to affert, has, under the peculiar circumftances of
Ireland, promoted rather than corrected the inconvenience of delegated government ; and has opened
rather than excluded the admiffion of abufe, which,
in fome degree, muft ever attend the exercife of
power in fituations removed from immediate inquiry
and control.

The firft object with the Chief-Governor in Ireland is to fecure the fupport of the Parliament, which
he finds exclufively exercifing all the powers of legifla-
tion.

tion. To gain the afcendancy in that affembly, and complete influence over its deliberations, becomes the fpring of all his efforts, and the application of all his power. The neceffity for this predominance over the free agency of Parliament, produced clearly by its disjunction from that of England, creates the imbecility of the Viceroy and the ftrength of paliamentary patronage, which fubjects him to infinite and increafing claims, in moft inftances detrimental to the Public, and difgraceful to the King's government. Hence has prevailed in Ireland an unprecedented fyftem of private jobbing and intrigue, and of unqualified public venality, in contempt of all character and opinion of the country. At no period was this practice carried higher, or was lefs artifice to conceal it from the view of the Public, than during the adminiftration of Lord Weftmoreland, whofe conduct, whatever reprehenfion it may deferve, derives fome extenuation not only from the general difficulty which every Chief Governor fuftains in managing the Irifh Legiflature, but from his meeting a confiderable parliamentary oppofition, and the occurrence of queftions of a delicate and difficult nature during his government. If it be afked, Since the conftitutions of both countries are the fame, and that prerogative and privilege, the rights of the King and the fubject, are extended on the fame policy, and defined within the fame limit in Ireland as in England, why fhould the King's government require extraordinary means of fupport in Ireland? and why fhould means be legitimated there which in England public opinion alone would render impracticable? this may be explained on general principle as well as by peculiar circum-. ftances in Ireland. It is more likely that the public bufinefs fhould be lefs obftructed, and be more eafily tranfacted in that country, where the fource and powers of Government are derived from the acts of its own people, where the national eftablifhment is of its own making in community of foil and birth, and where the nation has not to look beyond its

own

own limits for the original of the counsels which direct, and the authority which maintains the public order, than in that country where the efficacy of government is from abroad, and whose origin and creation are foreign and external. In the latter it is likely that a secret wish may prevail to disengage itself from this connexion, and render its government independent; and if the character of the people be impetuous and enterpising, turbulent and brave, and that nature has apparently supplied their country with the means and capacities of an independent state, it is almost a consequence in strict argument, or at least a probable inference, that a tendency should exist, and, as opportunities favour, display itself in open acts for effecting this separation. It will appear by and by, in the review of this subject, how far this general reasoning is confirmed in its application to Ireland, and whether she has, at any period, omitted an oppportunity of weakening her connexion with Britain. This effort to divide is a growing quantity, and must increase with the strength of one country and the difficulties of the other; besides the considerable addition it acquires from the progress of a false philosophy in politics, which flatters the passions of men, and estranges them from their governments. Hence arises the necessity, on the part of the executive, for more considerable influence in its administration of the dependent than of the superior country.

It has been objected to the constitution of England, that, however admirably it has adjusted the different powers of the state in mutual freedom, as well as in necessary co-operation, it has not sufficiently provided against an evil, which, under this fine theory, may produce despotism in practice; that the influence of the Crown is not entirely excluded from admission to the Legislature. Finely tempered as this constitution is between the popular form of government and the monarchical, partaking of the freedom of the one and the energy of the other, I am free to confess myself one of those who think it

one

one of the excellencies of that government, that the royal estate and the branches of the legislature are so connected, that the latter are open to the influence of the former; and to this do I ascribe the eminent solidity and firmness which, in an extraordinary manner, the British Government has manifested in these later years. In the midst of conspiracy at home, and an enlarged and tremendous foreign war, she has remained unshaken by the storm; and in the midst of the great deluge which has lately inundated the world, has appeared the only resting-place for religion and liberty: and the very acts of the British Parliament, which are adduced by popular prejudice, through the arts of the disaffected, as abuses of that influence, and as violences and injuries to the constitution, are the creatures of that necessity which the conspiracy of the external foe and the internal traitor had created; and to the timely interposition of these statutes is Great Britain, at the present moment indebted for salvation and existence.

There are several circumstances, however, which in England limit the extent of this influence, and secure to the public voice a decisive controul over the administration. In Ireland there are not these restraints; and as she is particularly constituted, her government is considerably less popular, and the influence of the executive is necessarily more extended and injurious, as to her interior, than in England. Since the separation of the Irish legislature from that of England, and Ireland becoming solely competent to direct her own internal government, no other link has remained to connect the two countries, but the influence of the English Minister in the Parliament of Ireland itself. Without this medium, it will appear that the coherence of the countries would be exposed to inevitable danger, as a strong principle of repulsion has unequivocally manifested itself in Ireland; and therefore, however it is to be regretted that the influence of the Crown in Ireland, or, more truly and properly, the name of the Crown, is made use of

of to produce and extend a fyſtem of corrupt afcen-
dency; yet it is confolation to an Engliſh fubject,
that it is of imperative neceſſity, ariſing from cauſes
for which Ireland alone is anſwerable. The conſtitu-
tional change of 1782 in Ireland threw the executive
at the mercy of her Parliament; which, as long as
it has the fole and excluſive power of legiſlation,
muſt command the liberality and enjoy the munifi-
cence of the Crown. Hence uniformly in Ireland,
fince the year 1782 particularly, parliamentary inte-
reſt has been the fole key to the favour of the Court;
all the honours and all the emoluments of the ſtate
have moved in the road of Parliament, the great
mart for their exchange. Without parliamentary
fupport, talent and virtue have been lame and impo-
tent in Ireland; they formed no claim to diſtinction
or reward: hence it has proceeded, that in general
the active and valuable offices at the bar, and in the
civil economy, have been filled by men whoſe talents
and capacities for their fituations were confiderably
inferior to very many of their cotemporaries. It
muſt be admitted, however, that in the ſhort adminiſtration of Lord Fitzwilliam, who vainly attempt-
ed a government by virtue, pre-eminent talents and
unblemiſhed reputation were raiſed to the heads of
the church and the univerfity; and your Excellency's
adminiſtration deferves confiderable praiſe for your
late promotion of a prelate, whoſe learning and ge-
nius, integrity of life, and amiability of manners, do
honour to your government.

The difference of extent, wealth, and importance
of the two countries, appears ſtrikingly in their par-
liaments. In England, charters of incorporation con-
ferring municipal privileges, and giving the elective
franchiſe, were gradually and occaſionally granted by
the Crown, as towns became refpectable and popu-
lous, and as commerce and manufacture flouriſhed.
Hence, notwithſtanding a few exceptions, and the
effects of the generation and decay, the advancement
and decline which attend every thing human, and af-
fect

fect communities as well as individuals, the English House of Commons is at present near a just representation of the great trading, manufacturing, and monied interests; but in Ireland, the House of Commons was framed in a great measure with the sole view of creating and securing Protestant ascendancy : its basis was not laid in the population, wealth, and importance of the kingdom, as was the case in England. Without reference to these characters, incorporating charters issued suddenly and numerously, for the mere purpose of procuring a Protestant majority; and hence appears to me to be derived the real cause of the great inequality of representation in the Irish Parliament : this great inequality has enabled an aristocracy to possess itself of the whole energy of Parliament, which in Ireland has been no more than the medium of its operation, and the instrument of its power. From the limited numbers of Commoners also in the lower House of Parliament it has been less difficult for the aristocracy to engross such an extent of borough patronage as should secure its parliamentary strength. A great inequality of property has uniformly prevailed in Ireland. The many rebellions there, with their consequent forfeitures, and the effects of the ancient division of the kingdom into numerous lordships and principalities, may have occasioned the very unequal division of land in Ireland. Whatever may have been its causes, it has generated and produced the aristocracy, and given it the means of parliamentary patronage.

In England, the strong tendency of its government was originally aristocratical. The monopoly of its soil produced a body of nobles who ruled both the King and the people; but the enterprises of commerce, and the industry of manufacture, raised the order of British commoners, which checked the influence of the barons, and supported the royal estate, which is allowed to be the origin of the popular part of the British constitution.

The magnitude of the English trade, the extent of her possessions, the qualities of her soil and the

faculties

faculties of her people, have produced such a capital of wealth and property as completely to countervail the landed proprietary : numerous trading companies and chartered societies for diverfified commerce, have eftablifhed fuch a monied intereft in England, as to make it the moft active and important rank in the ftate, as it refpects the great finews of its power, the national finances : hence the eafy and rapid alienation of her real property, which is ever varying its poffeffors. Thus the power of the Englifh commonalty increafes, and all ariftocratical tendencies and effects are obviated. To acquire an eftate becomes the ambition of the merchant ; the certainty of market and of felling for the value, induces to alienation, and multiplies the fellers, and whatever be the difadvantages of the national debt, the magnitude of the public ftocks has fo facilitated the means, and augmented the progrefs of private wealth, as to diffufe among the whole body of the people fuch a mafs of homogeneous property, that all claffes of Englifhmen not only feel themfelves without the collifion of oppofite views, and the contradictions of feparate rights, but combined and connected in one individual intereft, the fafety of the ftate ; but in Ireland none of thofe caufes have exifted, which in England have tempered the ariftocracy, and blended it in fine proportion with the rights of the people. Her fmall territorial extent is favourable to the growth of ariftocracy; her inconfiderable trade, her want of capital, and the perfect infancy of the nation in all the modes of induftry, and in all the acquifitions of wealth, have left the ariftocracy unbalanced. The centre of the conftitutional fyftem in Ireland wanting its due pofition, the whole vacillates and totters with infirmity. Not only the abfence of a monied intereft, and the want of a great mercantile power in Ireland, account for the inequality of her government ; but a pofitive caufe has exifted for ariftocratical tendency, which feems fully adequate to the effect.

The

The people of Ireland, in refpect to their religious relation, are divided in triple proportion of Catholics to Proteftants; and not only was the whole Catholic body, until very lately, excluded from the loweft participation in the legiflative and executive parts of government; but by the operation of fevere and impolitic penal ftatutes were precluded from the acquifition and enjoyment of property. It is not therefore a matter of wonder, that in fo fmall a country as Ireland, in which three-fourths of its population were depreffed by a weight of difability and penalties from rifing by talent or property in the ftate; the refidum of the people fhould have the nature and effect of an ariftocracy itfelf; that this faction fhould be itfelf capable of further reduction; and that, by monopoly and unjuft exclufion, an inconfiderable part may engrofs the power of the whole.

From the eafe alfo with which in a fmall country family connexion may fpread itfelf, the union of powerful men becomes ftrengthened by affinity, and confolidated by mutual intereft. Hence the combination of a few produces a formidable power, which in Ireland has had the maftery in public affairs. It has been openly avowed in the Irifh Parliament, that to break the ariftocracy, which impeded the King's government during the adminiftration of Lord Towfhend, coft the nation half a million fterling; and the kingdom was threatened with fimilar expence a few years ago, when fome parliamentary proprietors fhewed a difpofition to unite their forces, and turn their ftrength againft the government. Hence has proceeded the degree of corruption and the purfuit of private intereft, to the injury of the public, which have prevailed in Ireland; and the bufinefs of the Viceroy is hardly more than to appeafe the importunity, and fatisfy the cravings, of the ariftocracy. Frauds, peculations, and abufes of every kind, are protected from enquiry and fecured from punifhment. Boards of commiffion have been multiplied beyond the neceffity of the public bufinefs; and places have

been

been divided and granted for life, to oblige the greater number, and make them independent of the Government: and in the fame policy has prevailed the practice of reverfionary grants, to the injury of the fucceeding Viceroy, and the weakening of his adminiftration. Improvident bargains have been made with individuals in fraud to the Public; and in the fame fpirit of jobbing and venality the public buildings of Dublin have been raifed on fcites not only inconvenient, but highly ridiculous, and at im- menfe expenfe. Hence alfo the extravagant collec- tion of the public revenues, and a penfion lift in Ire- land, greater than in England, and above all, the proftitution of the peerage by actual fale, to the in- jury of merit, difhonour of the old nobility, and great odium of Government. This fhameful prac- tice of bringing to market the honours of the Crown, which cafts a deep fhade on the memory of Lord Weftmoreland in Ireland, has contributed more immediately and neceffarily to injure the public cha- racter of the Irifh Parliament, than any other affign-. able caufe. Under his government the Parliament call- ed in 1790, was compofed in an extraordinary man- ner; thofe wealthy Commoners who once filled the lower Houfe, and who had either acquired borough patronage, or in whofe families it had defcended with their eftates, were ennobled in the grofs, and trans- ferred to the upper houfe of Parliament, by which means the advowfon and inheritance of the Com- mons became vefted in the Lords, who for that turn gave up the prefentation to the Lord Lieutenant's fe- cretary. This unjuftifiable proceeding created an un- conftitutional dependency of the popular branch of the Legiflature on the ariftocratical; it promoted and avowed a fyftem of parliamentary traffic completely fufficient to difguft and alienate the Public; and the obvious confequence of this innovation was not only highly increafing the natural evil of the Irifh govern- ment in its tendency to ariftocracy, but, by remov- ing from the Houfe of Commons the men of confideration

deration and landed property, left it to a race of adventurers who were to make their way to situation and fortune by submissive and uniform servility to all the measures of the Court, or by affected patriotism to commence their parliamentary career in groundless and indiscriminate opposition to the Government, and afterwards with shameful apostacy, on the attainment of office, become advocates for the measures they had opposed, and panegyrists of the Government they had maligned. No assembly, however, could conduct itself with more public obsequiousness, or use a higher strain of adulation in all its addresses to the Chief Governor. This, however, is no more a proof of sincerity in public than in private life; for so long ago as the administration of the unfortunate Lord Strafford, they pronounced the highest encomiums on his conduct, and expressed their extraordinary obligations to their Sovereign for committing the government to so able and honest a servant, but a short time before their sending over to England articles of impeachment, and deputing commissioners to manage the prosecution of the unfortunate Earl. And so late as the year 1789, the very Parliament which had repeatedly and strongly expressed its loyalty and attachment to the King's person, and panegyrized his Viceroy, did, on the unfortunate occurrence of his malady, change their political creed; a great majority of Parliament deserted the cause of their Sovereign, and voted a public censure on the Chief Governor. However, as soon as the King's health appeared likely to be restored, and the powers of the state to continue in the same hands, they became as eager to repent as they had been to offend: so true a criterion of human conduct is private interest, and so fallible a pledge of sincerity is human profession.

The versatility of Parliament also on the Catholic question was most glaring; the recency of this transaction, however, precludes the necessity of particular statement: but the violent manner in which it resisted, and the

servility

fervility with which it foon afterwards conceded the Catholic claims, was fatal to the public intereft. It taught the people to look for redrefs of grievance, not by appeals to the Legiflature, but in the application of their own ftrength. Such has been the ftate of the Irifh Government, and fuch the caufes of that difcontent which has fo nearly been fatal to the empire.

The acknowledged independency of the Irifh Legiflature has prevented her concerns coming under the review of the Britifh Parliament; and there being no public medium of communication between the two countries, feems to me fufficiently to account for the ignorance which has prevailed in Britain of the real ftate of Ireland. A conftitution fo generative of abufe cannot continue; the fyftem of government which has prevailed in Ireland approaches to diffolution. It is the part of wifdom to forefee change, and to prevent or to improve it. That fomething muft be now done, cannot be controverted; either the Parliament of Ireland muft be new-fafhioned, or, as it is called, reformed, and the ariftocracy eradicated, or fhe muft be committed to the Parliament of England by fair and regular reprefentation. That, if the former take place, the dominion of England in Ireland muft determine, and the two countries be feparated, appears to me the obvious and moft neceffary confequence. This I fhall endeavour to eftablifh, and to communicate the ftrong perfuafion I feel, by reference to the hiftory of that country, to her late unfortunate rebellion, and the general ftate of politics. Sure I am that Ireland will find an union with England the panacea of her diforders, that it will convert her poverty into opulence, and her turbulence into tranquillity.

If a parliamentary reform be conceded to Ireland, no modification fhort of a pure democratic legiflature can have effect, To extinguifh, not to limit, the ariftocracy, is their great object: and the firft act of popular afcendancy would be the extermination of the fuperior order, to a moral certain-

ty

ty ; the fecond. would be the demolition of the
royal eftate, even if it had no foreign concern, but
were purely and folely exerciseable within the
kingdom. From the prefent ftate of the public
mind, in its long fermented diffatisfaction with its
Parliament, and from the political impreffions
which it has received from the American war and
the French. revolution, it is beyond doubt that if
the frame of Parliament be once innovated, it will
be rent from its very foundation, the whole efforts
of the people would be directed to the eftablifhing
of a democracy, and by every. poffible barrier to
exclude the influence of England and her counfels
from the affairs of Ireland; for, the hiftory of the
late rebellion. as it is fpread upon parliamentary
record, and of the proceedings of the difcontented
and difaffected in Ireland for fome years, prepara-
tory to their coming to open war with the Government, eftablifh it to the conviction of every man,
that feparation from England was the prime and
the grand object; a reform in the Parliament of
Ireland was to be the means, and the decifive ftep
towards the attainment of the former : a more
equal reprefentation of the people, therefore, re-
founded on every fide, as the demand of the nation
upon its Government. Under this fpecious pretext was concealed the hoftile difpofition towards
Great Britain. The body of the people looked no
farther than the mere queftion of reform, which
the general conduct of Parliament appeared to
render not only reafonable but neceffary; but its.
real end, and the great fcheme of change and independence, were referved to a few, and lurked in
the dark receffes of confpiracy and treafon, until
the fullnefs of time and the fuccefs of the auxilia-
ry meafures fhould call for the open avowal of the
great object, and its publication to the nation.
Thus the rafhnefs of the unthinking and the faith
of the credulous are ever expofed to the fubtlety
of the wicked, who enlifts them as inftruments of
his caufe and accomplices in his crimes.

. That the connexion between the two countries
has

has been weakened, and that the public conduct of Ireland has, upon some great occasions, facilitated and promoted the means of separation, will appear from the particular consideration and effect of two remarkable instances, independent of the general review of her history. In the year 1782, a constitutional change was effected in Ireland, the most important which had occurred since her annexation to Great Britain: before that period she formed a more immediate and connected member of the the British empire, under the direct influence and care of the general government. The regulations of her interior, as well as her external relations, were matter on which the English Parliament might act; and the power in the Government of England, as well of original approbation of the general measure, as of its final sanction in detail, protected the people of Ireland from the misconduct and abuses of its own Parliament. This direct and open controul of the English Government over the affairs of Ireland, the dependency of the Irish army on the English mutiny act, and the limited capacity and circumscribed authority of the Irish Parliament, necessarily connected and preserved Ireland, in conjunction with Great Britain. During this time, notwithstanding the measured and subordinate power of the Irish Parliament, it was more respectably constituted than ever it has been since. It was composed almost entirely of men of fortune, whose situations did not expose them to the prostitution of public character, nor chalk out a line of personal aggrandisement through the windings of political intrigue, at the public expence: Ireland did not then feel the great financial pressure which the necessity of parliamentary purchase has since created; she then knew nothing of that common speculation which since has filled the benches of Parliament with numerous and successive adventurers; and Ireland was then equally ignorant of the market for nobility, and that extensive and extravagant system of influence which kept the voice and wants of the Public unheard

and

and unheeded. But in 1782 the great link of empire which connected the two countries, gave way,
and nothing remained after the renunciation of the
British Barliament to fecure the union of the
crowns, but the covered and fatal medium of fecret
influence in the eftablifhment of an expenfive and
growing patronage to counteract the acquired independence and improved capacity of the Irifh Parliament. The caufes of this extraordinary occurrence, the ftate of the puplic mind in Ireland at
that time, and the means by which this great conftitutional change was effected, fhall be briefly
ftated, that the whole defign and full intentions of
thofe who moved and led the politics of Ireland
may be difclofed and made manifeft.

The war with America had produced confiderable effects, not only in the Britifh empire, but
through Europe: it threw a falfe and delufive glare
over modern politics, inftead of a fober and falutary
light. Hence fome have derived the convulfions
of France, and the meteor which has fcared and
diftracted Ireland. It is certain, however, that
the peculiar nature of the conteft between Britain
and her colonies provoked every where and emi-
nently in Ireland, much diffufed converfation and
general difcuffion on the principles of government.
Perhaps at no time, not even at the revolution of
1688, were the abftract rights of the people more
fully examined, or the general theory of civil efta-
blifhments more accurately analyfed; and it is
certain that the inftitution of the tranf-atlantic
empire, under the circumftances and manner of
its original, has given new character and complexion to the politics of Europe: of thefe politics Ireland had in a great degree partaken. The
nature of her connexion with England, the ftate
of her Parliament, and the national obfcurity,
were topics which engroffed the public attention,
and on which the talents of the ftate were em-
ployed. It need not be inquired, what was the
refult of the public inveftigation on the queftion,
whether actual force of arms, acquifition in war,

or

or real and implied compact, was the foundation
of the Englifh dominion in Ireland. To argue
againft the pride or intereft of your adverfary, is
as vain among nations as among individuals. A
difcuffion of this queftion would be now irrevelant;
the prefent occafion calls for no fuch inquiry;
a temperate, difpaffionate, and calm confideration
of the prefent ftate of Ireland, with the light re-
flected from her hiftory, and her late tranfactions
alone, is neceffary at this important moment. In
the American war, armed in her own defence
againft the common enemy, Ireland feized the
favourable opportunity of her own ftrength, and
the imbecility of England, to confirm by decifive
acts thofe argumentative conclufions, which to
her mind had refuted the claims and rights of England, and eftablifhed her own title to independence; to diffolve all other connexion than with
the crown of Great Britain; became the great object of Ireland, for which fhe prepared to make
every effort, and apply her whole force. In the
crifis of minifterial weaknefs, the great conceffion
was made. After a mighty amputation of empire,
it feemed prudent by any means to preferve the
remainder; and England not only yielded the
future independence of Ireland, but, in her ftate
of durefs and neceffity, renounced her former title:
fhe remitted the poffeffion, and confeffed herfelf a
diffeifor. The fatal confequences which followed
the denial to America of fharing the Britifh conftitution, hurried the Englifh minifter into com-
pliance with the demands of Ireland, in their full
and unlimited extent. Had he been guided by
true policy, and had he fufficiently diftinguifhed
the cafe of Ireland from that of America, the
neceffity of the prefent difcuffion would not have
arifen, nor fhould the Public have been troubled
with this addrefs.

The tranfaction in 1782 is particularly dwelt
on, becaufe it furnifhes a clear demonftration that
the conftitutional change which was demanded
and effected, was not becaufe it was the moft fui-
ted

ted to the neceffities of Ireland, but becaufe the Irifh
nation had been inflamed by every art to view the
connexion with England as injurious to her honour and detractive of her national character.
The object was more to fhake off the dependency
of the kingdom on the Englifh Legiflature, than
any enlarged view of the future interefts of Ireland. It was a queftion of pride more than of
policy, and it is not the character of pride to
refpect its real interefts.

The full principle of the conftitutional change
of 1782 became the bafis of a moft important
tranfaction in 1789, at the lamentable period of
the King's indifpofition. The *patriots* in Ireland,
and the great movers of her *politics*, on this occafion gave full fcope to their zeal for the *unity* of
the Britifh empire, and their attachment to its
combined interefts : they contended, that, on the intermiffion of the royal functions, Ireland, as an
imperial independent nation, was exclufively competent to provide for this emergency; that the two
countries had no other union than in their executive; and therefore, that in every poffible cafe
of its fufpenfion or determination, the Parliament
of Ireland alone was adequate to the great imperial duty of fupplying the vacant power. By a
free election of a royal fiduciary, to hold the King's
prerogative in truft for themfelves only, under
fuch limitations as they fhould define its exercife;
and indeed the argument went the whole length
of eftablifhing, that, on fuch an occafion, the
Parliament of Ireland might take the executive
into their own hands, or altogether difcontinue
the royal eftate. And had it not been for the ac-
cidental fympathy of the parliamentary oppofition
in both countries, this abftract argument would
probably have had a decifive practical effect in the
delegation of the royal authority to a regent not
deriving under the Parliament of England: in
which event an actual feparation muft have taken
place, as there would not have remained a parti-
cle of connexion between the two countries. Their
con-

conduct, however, and proceedings, on this trying occasion, demonstrate the danger which threatens the empire: it establishes the tendency of Ireland to separation; and that on the present constitutional footing of these kingdoms no barrier is formed to prevent its effect. It is clear also, that, without seeking for it, an opportunity may arise again of vacancy in the Crown, or its intermission; that Ireland may again feel herself called upon to exercise the imperial right by the spontaneous occurrence of public circumstances, without any arbitrary or uncalled for discussion of her right; and it is manifest, that, on such an occasion, her conduct would not be regulated by the interests and policy of the empire. The parliamentary report of the late rebellion also proves incontestibly, that, since the year 1789, the principle of separation has gained rapidly, that it has wonderfully increased under the mere influence of general political impression made by the French revolution, without the actual interference of the French government in the affairs of Ireland, the intrigues of her emissaries, or her systematic and authorized abominations. And the conduct of the Irish Parliament in 1789 shows, that the influence of England in the Irish Legislature, through the medium of its patronage, forms a very frail and precarious combination. The shameful tergiversation of the Irish members, at that time, must convince that the honour of individuals is no security on which to repose the strength and happiness of the British empire.

From the first records of her history, Ireland has been particularly and specially distinguished for domestic dissension and division: Before her connexion with England, during her old government, if the term be not much abused in this application of it, the kingdom was subjected to numerous principalities and authorities, which carried on with each other incessant and implacable wars. The wildness of uncorrected nature marked the face of the country: as savagery

ry unfoftened and unhumanized their manners
and practices in war, traces of hoftile incurfion
were every where manifeft; and plains, to which
Nature had not denied fertility, mouldered into
bogs and moraffes. In the violence of civil ftrife,
no peaceful improvement could be effected. In
the divifion of governments there was nothing national; and thence, as all things fublunary tend
to degeneracy and decay, unlefs fuftained and re-
cruited by collateral aid, the want of culture de-
teriorated the foil, as the abfence of civil difcip-
line ftill farther brutalized the national manners.

On the arrival of the Britons in Ireland, in the
year 1172, every thing manifefted to them a country deeply funk in the mifery of ignorance and
barbarifm. Before the connexion with England,
therefore, neither commerce nor manufacture
could have exifted, or any one work of public
utility been devifed or executed; and fince that
connexion, though in that great length of time
Ireland has naturally improved in many important
refpects, and that this improvement has arifen
entirely from her communication with England,
and in its direct proportion; yet, in every period
almoft has fhe had her tranquillity interrupted by
general rebellion or local rifings, and has ever
been the prey of civil and religious diffenfions.
This continual difturbance and uncertainty of the
public condition in Ireland has counteracted her
natural advantages, and prevented that enlarged
intercourfe with England, which would have extended her trade, and affimilated the national
manners to the fobriety and fubordination of the
Englifh character. The truth of thefe pofitions
will appear eftablifhed by the following brief review of the Irifh hiftory.

Henry the Second acquired the dominion of
Ireland as much by his high reputation for juftice
as a king and wifdom as a legiflator as by the terror of his arms. The piratical depredations of
the Irifh on his Englifh fubjects, their cruel treat-
ment of prifoners of war, and the military levies
which

which his enemy the French King was enabled to make in Ireland, confiderably induced the Englifh monarch to fanction with his own authority and prefence the private adventures of his fubjects. It is remarkable that the fame policy fhould fo ftrongly apply at this day for permanently uniting and preferving that which Henry the Second thought it fo neceffary to acquire. The politic piety of the times juftified this expedition of Henry by a papal bull, confecrating the title of conqueft for the great end of civilization and religion. Almoft all the native princes, who were very numerous, fubmitted to the King, did homage, and took the oaths of fidelity and allegiance. Voluntary fubmiffions, however, were not more effectual and fincere at that time than they are now. The Englifh colony planted in Leinfter was fubject to every kind of outrage, and the utmoft cruelty characterized its barbarous enemies : their continual aggreffions, and the commotions of the country, determined the unfortunate Richard the Second on two royal voyages to Ireland. The force with which he was attended in his firft, fpread terror and confternation; fo that, as the hiftorians of thefe times obferve, the Irifh had recourfe to a policy, which they often practifed with fuccefs, to divert the blow which they could not fuftain. With feigned acknowledgments of paft tranfgreffions and infincere affurances for the future, all the powerful leaders of the Irifhry waited upon the King at his arrival, with fubmiffion and fealty; and the Earl Marfhal was empowered by fpecial commiffion to receive homage and repetitions of fidelity from the Irifhry of Leinfter, which they rendered on their knees, and were afterwards admitted to the kifs of peace; and in like manner the King himfelf received the fubmiffion of Ulfter. However, as foon as Richard had departed, and the military force was diffolved, this humility was renounced, and, in violation of facred engagements, the public peace was again interrupted, and the borders of the Englifh pale again fuffered the ravages of war.

It

It is obfervable, that this perfidious quality, which furmounts all religious barrier, and violates all focial principle, has continued characteriftical of the lower Irifh to this hour. In the late rebellion, an enlightened and merciful policy proclaimed pardon and protection; but the very wretches who availed themfelves of the benignity of Government, in many inftances, have fince been apprehended in the commiffion of new crimes, and the perpetration of greater enormities. So permanent muft be the qualities of men, to whom the improvements of life do not defcend, and whofe political place debars them from any fhare in the general civilization.

From the reign of Richard the Second to that of Elizabeth was one continued feries of difturbance; but in her reign the moft formidable and dangerous rebellion occurred of any fince the reduction of Ireland. The rebels having had the aid of foreign power, the Spaniards effected a landing in Kinfale, and their ftandard was foon joined by feveral of the Irifh lords, particularly by the Earls Tyrone and Tyrconnell, who had marched from the North at the head of a confiderable army; but being engaged by the Lord Deputy Mountjoy, were entirely defeated. The Spaniards fubmitted on the terms of leaving the kingdom; and the rebellious Lord Tyrone experienced the fame merciful indulgence, which, to the immortal honour of Great Britain, has continued to this day her peculiar character, and to which your Excellency's conduct from the commencement of your government has given the ftrongeft atteftation. Lord Tyrone was received to fubmiffion and mercy; and in 1606, King James iffued a commiffion of grace for confirming the poffeffions of the Irifh againft all claims of the Crown arifing from the attainder of thofe concerned in the rebellion. From this royal clemency and moft gracious favour, a perfect fettlement of the kingdom might have been expected, as no fmall foundation feems to have been laid for the return of general tranquility

quility. However, nothing could reduce to focial order and fubordination minds fo ferocious and
intractable: for at that very time, an impunity
for rebellion, thefe fame Earls Tyrone and Tyrconnell, and almoft all the Irifhry of Ulfter, were
engaged in a new confpiracy to provoke a general rifing, feize the caftle of Dublin; and, for
the accomplifhment of thefe nefarious purpofes,
had actually folicited foreign aid. The fame
Providence, however, which at this day preferves
and favours the Britifh empire, defeated this confpiracy.

A furprifing parallel runs through all the tranfactions of the Irifh hiftory, which feem to partake
the fame fpirit, and continue the fame character.
The trial of Henry and John Shears, convicted in
July laft, records a fcheme of treafon wonderfully fimilar, though more artfully laid and more ex-
tenfively diffufed. In both, the firft facrifice of
rebellion was to be the King's reprefentative and
council; the Englifh minifters and all the fup-
porters of Englifh councils were to be devoted
to the fury of the mob, and become the firft vic-
tims for eftablifhing the acquired independence.

The rebellious Lords having fled beyond fea,
made violent complaints abroad, that they had
been driven from home for matter of religion, and
with great injuftice as to their claims and preten-
fions; on which the King thought proper to make
a declaration, which was publifhed through Europe.
But in the late rebellion, the full and free confef-
fions of the principal traitors have prevented the
fuccefsful repetition of this artifice. Befides the
convictions and outlawries had againft the actors
in thefe rebellions, there was a general attainder
by the ftatute of the 11th of King James, by which
500,000 acres of land in the north of Ireland were
forfeited to the Crown, which enabled the King to
make that Proteftent plantation in Ulfter which has
become thefeat of the only manufacture in Ireland,
and continues to be diftinguifhed in a very great
degree above the reft of the kingdom for its induftry, wealth, and population, though in quality of

foil much below the average fertility of the kingdom : a plain and irrefragable proof of the advan-
tage which Ireland has derived from her connexion
with England, to whom, whatever improvement
she has acquired since the days of her King Dermot,
must certainly be referred : which obfervation appears to be justified still farther, by the superior
order and improvement of the hither coast of Ireland to the farther. The western division of Ireland is more purely Irish, which may have proceeded from the policy of Cromwell, who forced
the ancient and native families to residence beyond
the Shannon ; and though those parts of Ireland,
originally of English settlement, were perhaps the
most disloyal and disaffected in the late rebellion,
yet it must be remembered, that colonial establish-
ments but seldom have had the merit of filial gra-
titude ; and though the north of Ireland partook
largely of the late conspiracy, yet she preserved
her tranquility in a much greater degree than the
zeal and ardour of the rebel leaders to make her
the great reservoir of treason gave foundation to
expect : nor was her conduct in the midst of the
rebellion stained with those enormities which were
committed in the other parts of the kingdom ;
and which, for the honour of humanity, and pity
for that unfortunate nation, ought not to be particularly stated : but it is matter of duty to read to
the world the great lesson of misfortune and pu-
nishment which are sure to follow the commission
of crimes.

It may be further observed, with respect to the
north of Ireland, that the circumstances of her
prosperity and her superior opulence formed the
temptation for her seduction ; that the less important parts of the kingdom might more easily
take the example of infidelity. The religious per-
suasion also which prevails in the North having peculiar partiality to republicanism, facilitated and
predisposed that country to measures which mani-
festly tended to gratify their favourite principle.

From

From the rebellion of Tyrone until the year 1641, Ireland appeared to have enjoyed general tranquillity ; the interefts which divided, and the animofities which irritated, the different defcriptions of her inhabitants, appeared to have been fucceeded by union, fraternity, and peace. The new poffeffors of lands had diligently applied to their cultivation, and the much calumniated adminiftration of Lord Strafford had made great progrefs in the general improvement of the kingdom : thefe appearances, however, were delufive ; more extenfive mifchief was in preparation, which the intermiffion of actual hoftility gave leifure to improve and mature.

Among the reafons and caufes which are affigned for this rebellion, is the great change of property which had taken place in Ulfter after the forfeitures of the fix countries under the act of James ; and probably in the relentlefs temper of the Irifh, the jealoufy of property which they had forfeited was peculiarly inveterate. The afcendancy of Proteftantifm and theEnglifh intereft, which each defeat had promoted, were without doubt the great and leading caufes of the rebellion of 1641, which, for indifcriminate and fhocking murders, had no precedent. The unfortunate fituation of the Englifh monarch, the difaffection of his parliament, and particularly the fuccefsful rebellion of his fubjects in North Britain, gave occafion and opportunity to the execution of the defign. The Irifh leaders faw clearly that a favourable moment had arrived for terminating the Englifh dominion in Ireland ; and that one great effort, no matter in in what way, would give emancipation to their country. The embarraffment of the King's government, and the difpofition of the Britifh Parliament, augmenting inftead of removing public diforder, gave confidence to the caufe, and infpired high hopes of eafy and rapid victory. The defign, however, againft the capital was difcovered ; the firft object of the rebels failed, but through the
king-

kingdom a maſſacre commenced too horrid to be dwelt upon.

The forts and garriſon-towns were aſſailed, and the kingdom was ſhaken to its centre. The reſtitution of property, the domination of the Catholic religion, and deliverance from Engliſh ſupremancy, were the great and ſacred objects which were to ſanctify, by their attainment, the wickedneſs of the means. Such were the inducements to lead, and ſuch the hopes to animate the family of the ancient proprietor, the ignorant and bigotted crowd, and the numerous claſs of Lords and Princes who delighted in the ambition, but felt not the miſeries of private war. The idea ſuccefsfully propagated at that time among the body of the people was the danger of their religon ; they were made to believe that the Engliſh Parliament had determined on the abolition of Popery in Ireland, and that the Scots were to be the zealous inſtruments of this perſecution. There was no foundation for this alarm ; the ignorance, credulity, and ſuperſtition of the lower Iriſh, made it unneceſſary : they were already diſpoſed to the moſt unfavourable ſuſpicions of thoſe whom, under the influence of long and ſyſtematic deluſion, they had been made to conſider as enemies. The aſcendency of Preſbyterianiſm, and the influence of the Scots, at that time gave colour and pretext to the fears and inſinuations which the deceiver was every where ſuggeſting. The moſt violent animoſities raged between the churches of Rome and Scotland, which confirmed every fear and magnified every danger which the credulity of one might apprehend from the fanaticiſm of the other. The diviſions between theſe bodies of men in doctrine and affection were extreme, inveterate, and implacable : ſo wonderfully does man pervert the beneficence of his God in educing diſcord, and creating differences, from the very religion which came from heaven to harmonize and unite. The leaders found in this prejudice of the people
the

the direct key to infurrection, which at this hour locks up the minds of the lower Irifh, or opens them to rebellion. The leaders of the late con-fpiracy adopted the clue of their predeceffors in 1641, and with the fame fatal effect. After this great lapfe of time, the common people in Ire-land are found equally credulous and bigotted; they were made lately to believe, that the Catho-lic religion was in imminent danger, and that its perfecution impended from that government, which fince the acceffion of the King, has breathed the mildeft influence on fectaries of every denomina-tion, and which has not only tolerated the Catho-lic fubject, but removed, the reftraints of former times, and given him conftitutional rank.

The Prefbyterian not having now afcendancy in the ftate, and being fraternized with the Catho-lic, the artifice of 1641 could not be repeated; fome new object therefore was to alarm, fome new enemy to be fuggefted ; and the common peo-ple of Ireland were impreffed with conviction that certain focieties which arofe in the North, and afterwards were formed throughout the kingdom for the protection of their families and properties, had been actually commiffioned by the Govern-ment to put down the Catholic faith ; under which pretence, and moft wicked and groundlefs infinuation, were the Catholics raifed, as it were, to protect their altars from profanation, and af-fail the public authority by force of arms. It muft be remembered alfo, that as the misfor-tunes of Charles the Firft, and the diftractions of the Britifh Government, marked the period of the rebellion in 1641, the confpiracy of 1798 was formed and carried into effect, when Great Britain was involved in a war the moft difficult, varied, and extenfive fhe ever waged, and when the enemy fhe had to combat was the moft active, infidious, and deadly ; and that in co-operation aad confede-racy with that enemy, the Irifh rebels laid their fcheme of maffacre and ruin.

From

From the extinction of the rebellion in 1641, by the force and perseverance of Cromwell, we come to the period of the Revolution. The unconstitutional acts and superstitious bigotry of the House of Stuart had removed it from the throne of England ; which removal, by the law of England, and an express act of the Irish Legislature, equally applied to Ireland : but the superstition of James found adherents in the ignorance of the Irish, and all those who wished the separation of the countries were united in his cause. The rivalry of the Catholic and Protestant was this time at its height ; and as the former had predominated much in Ireland, and the Revolution established the ascendancy of the latter religious as well as political considerations insured the abdicated Monarch the support of Ireland ; and though loyalty and affection for the House of Stuart may be advanced to justify the conduct of the Irish, and that attachment to the reigning family is highly meritorious ; yet it is too plain, that it was the religion of James, and not his relation to the throne of England, which recommended him to Ireland. The British Legislature, on true and sound constitutional principles, alone was competent to create and supply the vacancies of the throne ; and by the express provisions of statutes in both nations, the sovereignty of Ireland necessarily and immediately followed that of Great Britain ; and therefore, by adherence to the House of Stuart, after the determination of the English Parliament, Ireland broke her constitutional engagagements, and divided herself from the empire.

It is true, that the then chief governor of Ireland, Lord Tyrconnell, who was also at the head of the army, and a very considerable number of persons in official stations under the Government, were in the interests of James, and bore arms in his support ; and that, however great and national the question then at issue was, affection to a family long in possession, and the violence to old prejudice in its sudden expulsion, and

sub-

fubftitution of a foreigner, all amount, in a great
degree, to excufe and extenuate the conduct of
Ireland in its refiftance to the new government,
which appears from the conduct of King William
himfelf, who carried on the war in Ireland not as
with traitors and rebels, but as with fair and ligiti-
mate enemies; yet important inftruction is con-
veyed to us by thefe tranfactions, which fuggeft
the imperative neceffity of now fixing the conftitutional relation of the two countries in fuch a way,
that it fhall ever be underftood, and put beyond
controverfy, that Ireland cannot in any cafe decide, or at all difcufs the queftion of title to the
common executive of thefe kingdoms; that her
crown cannot be feparately confidered, or abftract-
edly become the fubject of public argument; but
that, to every poffible purpofe, there is a legal and
conftitutional merger of it in that of Great Britain.
And it is manifeft, that, as long as human affairs
proceed in their natural progrefs, great occafions
may arife, in which the policy or liberties of Great
Britain may require, that the rights of perfons
claiming title to her crown, fhould be modified, and
even extinguifhed; and, that as long as Ireland
fhall have a feparate legiflature, fhe will have the
means of difcuffion and determination of fuch rights;
fhe will have no phyfical impediment to the exercife of her own free will; and as to her propriety
in its exercife, that will depend on the views, public and individual, of the members of her legiflature. Speculations of the probable nature of her
public carriage in thofe trials, will be confiderably
aided by reference to her hiftory, and all her former
conduct; and as the moft aggravated evils peculiarly attend difputes and contefts for royal fuccef-
fion; and that in Ireland there would be religious
difcord to add to their inveteracy; it neceffarily
refults from enlarged and humane policy, that Ire-

D   land

land fhould not, by the form of her government, be left expofed to the intrigues of the royal claimant, who fhould happen to be disfranchifed and depofed; and that a way fhould not be left open which muft lead to her own convulfion, and the diftreffes of the empire.

In the reign of William, the queftion of the dependency of Ireland, and the authority of the Englifh Parliament to interfere in her concerns, to the exclufion of her own legiflature, was publicly agitated. In 1644, the power of binding Ireland by an Englifh ftatute was argued on legal grounds by Sir Richard Bolton, and ably anfwered by Serjeant Mayart; both arguments may be feen in Harris's Hibernica. The oppofition which uniformly had been made in Ireland to the dominion of England, now openly queftioned and denied the control of her legiflature. Soon after the Revolution, feveral acts had paffed in England, in which Ireland was exprefsly named and included. To obviate the effect of thefe ftatutes, and eftablifh their incompetence to bind Ireland, her Parliament tranfmitted acts of their own, enacting and confirming the matter of the Britifh ftatutes; and in 1698 an ingenious writer publifhed a fubtle and popular refutation of the claims of England, in which he freely and openly contended for the freedom of the Irifh Parliament. But, to my conception, a great part of the general doctrine and argument of Mr. Molyneux tends as ftrongly to difprove the authority of the Englifh Crown, as of its Parliament, over Ireland; but whether his reafoning was legitimate or not, was immaterial; it became the ftandard of political orthodoxy in Ireland.

The Englifh Commons, however, were attentive to the public intereft. There then exifted no national difficulties or embarraffment to extort from them conceffions repugnant to the conftitution of

the

the empire. They addreſſed the throne on the pernicious aſſertions of this publication, and the dangerous tendency of the late conduct of the Iriſh Parliament; and aſſured the King of their determination to maintain and preſerve, in a parliamentary way, the dependence and ſubordination of Ireland to the imperial crown of the realm.

In the reign of Anne and George, the rival claims of the throne of England, and the prevalent Catholiciſm of Ireland, produced ſeveral acts of Parliament, certainly of a very penal nature, againſt perſons of the Romiſh communion. The Revolution was the era of Britiſh liberty; it undermined the antiquated and prieſtly notions of paſſive obedience and hereditary right, and uſhered into theſe kingdoms a ſober, ſalutary, rational, and uſeful freedom The Catholic religion had connected itſelf with theſe political errors, and was the faith of the baniſhed Monarch and his adherents in both kingdoms. And hence in England aroſe the neceſſity of diſcouraging, by civil diſabilities, a profeſſion of men, whoſe doctrines were hoſtile to its new civil arrangement, and whoſe minds were attached to the fortunes of a family whoſe claims of power were incompatible with the political and religious liberty of England But the popery laws in Ireland were marked with peculiar and inconceivable ſeverity. Not only the reaſons for thoſe acts of penalty which exiſted in England applied to Ireland; but there were others peculiar to herſelf, which ſharpened her reſentment, and produced a ſeries of ſtatutes by no means creditable to her legiſlative code. A very conſiderable change had taken place in the poſſeſſion of lands in Ireland, in conſequence of repealed forfeitures, and particularly the immenſe confiſcation which followed the triumph of the Houſe of Orange in 1688, when 1,0᳟0,000 plantation acres fell to the diſpoſal of the Crown; ſo that in Ireland the

jealouſy

jealoufy of property was added to the virulence of
her religious diffenfion. Befides, the great difpro-
portion of Catholic to Proteftant made it alfo neceffary to fupply paucity of numbers by additional mu-
niments from the legifiature ; and indeed the meafures of the Irifh Parliament during this period
went the whole extent that the moft jealous proprietary or moft bigoted fanatic could require for the
fecurity of their acquired lands, and the afcendancy
of the Proteftant faith. We have lived, however,
to fee a complete feparation of divinity and politics,
and the country of the Moft Catholic King become
the metropolis of irreligion and paganifm ; the triple crown has fallen, and by means of that very
power, whofe head once gloried in being eldeft fon
of the church, the fame nation whofe enthufiaftic
Chriftianity once covered the Eaft with her legions,
now embraces the infidelity fhe then perfecuted,
and paganifes the land fhe went to reclaim. The
Houfe of Stuart is no more ; its misfortunes are
nearer our recollection than its power. The rights
of property in Ireland are confirmed by length of
time, by prefcription, by alienation, and acquiefcence.

The proportion of numbers in Ireland between
Catholic and Proteftant is now much varied in favour of the latter ; hence the penal laws have fur-
vived the neceffity which created them, and the
reafoning by which they were juftified. The danger to modern government arifes, not from the
theory of religionifts, but from the enemies of all
religion ; and therefore the laws which neceffity and
prudence demand for the prefervation of government, and the fecurity of the public, fhould have
a free and general operation ; not applying to dif-
tinct defcriptions of fubjects, but making one divifion only, that of the juft and unjuft ; that all may
. be

be enjoined the great precept of religion and policy —Fear God, and honour the King.

In 1719 the Irish House of Peers asserted a right of final judicature over all judgments and decrees given in courts within the kingdom, and committed to the custody of their Black Rod the Barons of the Exchequer, who, in opposition to their order, enforced the decree of the English Peers in the case of Annesley and Sherlock. This attempt produced the act of George the First, which declares, that the Irish Lords have not the appellant jurisdiction, and again repeats the dependency of the Crown of Ireland, and the supremacy of the British Parliament.

In 1751 an appropriated surplus remained in the Irish Treasury, which the Duke of Dorset, then Lord Lieutenant, consented, in the King's name, to apply to the discharge of the national debt. The Irish Parliament forbore stating in the act which they transmitted, this previous consent of the Crown: the clause, however, was introduced in England, and afterwards received in Ireland with much dissatisfaction, as it was insisted there, that their own Parliament was competent to appropriate the residuum without the King's previous consent, notwithstanding that the King had an independent hereditary revenue in Ireland, and that the surplus in the Exchequer resulted as well from the branches of that revenue as from any other parts of the public income; which is a power that the Parliament of England, under similar circumstances, could not claim against the Crown. And in 1753, on the recurrence of this question, the amended act from England was rejected. However, the prerogative of the Crown was vindicated, and the money was issued at the Treasury under the authority of a King's letter only.—These distinct facts, at different periods in the history of Ireland, are enumerated to shew the rise and growth of a disposition for

weakening

weakening the connection with Britain, and establishing an independent government.

The circumstances which follow, which have occurred in the present reign, admit of no equivocal construction, and establish important conclusions.

In 1778, during the dissensions of Great Britain with her American colonies, petitions and claims of rights were set on foot among the people of Ireland at that time, of a commercial nature only ; these, however, grew in extent, and the public demand became louder, as difficulties abroad and discontents at home embarrassed the King's government. This clamour had its effect ; and what was called a free trade was conceded by the British Parliament

Whenever the public mind is inflamed by the agitation of political questions, which are first advanced by a few of more sagacity than virtue, whose private pursuits are masked under the appearance of public interest, the concession of the national request will not allay the ferment, or extinguish the fire which consumes the public peace. Another grievance calls for redress, or some new privilege is suggested, more important than the former ; and without which, it is said, the state cannot exist. Thus concession leads to new demands, and the public appetite grows with what it devours.

The attainment of commercial advantages in extension of trade and removal of restraints, was followed immediately by demands of a constitutional nature, which went to change the frame of government altogether. It was insinuated that freedom of trade could be secured only by independence in the government : and the imposing analogy was advanced, that as, with the individual, he will not be industrious unless the fruits of his labour be secured, so the capital of a nation will not expend itself in commerce or manufacture, unless it has the sole power of its regulation. The transition therefore from
the

the fubject of trade to that of government was natural and eafy; but as the latter goes more to the
feelings of men over whom pride has more dominion
than intereft, a greater degree of union and earneft-
nefs prevailed in Ireland upon this queftion than on
the former. The nation at length became extremely
agitated; armed affociations covered the land, whofe
origin was for the meritorious defence of their country againft the common enemy.

The extent and multiplied demands of the war
in which Britain was then engaged had much redu-
ced the military eftablifhment in Ireland; and her
coaft having been more than once infulted by the
enemy, the government could not but applaud the
voluntary exertions of thofe who came forward in
the public fervice. Nothing, however, can fhow
more the want of ftrength, or the want of wifdom
of the government at that time, in fuffering a large
military force to rife in the country, totally inde-
pendant of its authority. Long experience has
fhown, that the beft inftitutions of human wifdom
are fubject to abufe, and that good and evil are fo
intimately compounded, and fo infenfibly diftribu-
ted in all the allotments of human life, that nothing
can be faid to be abfolutely good which may not
partake of evil; and no meafure to be fo conveni-
ent from which mifchief may refult. Had the volunteers of Ireland adhered to their firft principles,
and kept in view the object of their affociation, their
conduct would have been beyond all praife. Whenever the neceffities of our country oblige us to af-
fume a military character, it fhould be well underftood, and never for a moment forgotten, that the
exercife of civil rights is fufpended; it is for their
final prefervation that the foldier is created, who
may be called the great executive of the ftate, while
it is the citizen who legifl ates; and as thefe two
great powers of will and action, of command and
performance,

performance, cannot combine in the state without despotism, neither can they concentrate in the individual without producing anarchy. No principle of the British constitution can be so clearly proved, none is more suitable to its wisdom, and certainly none, in its application, contributes more to the tranquility, to the liberties, and to the happiness of the state.

The volunteers of Ireland, from soldiers became politicians, and formed a military convention, in perfect mimicry of the forms of Parliament, at the very moment when the lawful government was in the exercise of its functions. Such was the state of public affairs; the intended effect was produced, and the British Parliament renounced all dominion and authority within the kingdom of Ireland.

The continued practice of popular conventions, and of arbitrary, self-formed associations in Ireland, for discussing and resolving on abstract questions of government, for exploring defects and suggesting innovations in the constitution, have been highly detrimental, and have palpably contributed to the origin, formation, and systematic progress of the late rebellion. When it is considered that these questions are in their nature the most difficult; that erroneous notions concerning them are most dangerous; that the bulk of society is not competent; from learning, experience, or judgment, to treat of them; that the few who have capacity may want integrity and virtue; it is clear, that such societies are most likely to become pernicious instruments of sedition and treason, instead of a medium for enlightening and improving the Public. And hence well-regulated states have annexed conditions of age and property to the members of the legislature, that its deliberations may be directed by the wisdom which results from years and education, and secured by the virtue which dwells with independence.

independence. The Convention Act of the prefent Chancellor in Ireland prevents all popular meetings by election and delegation. The licentioufnefs of original focieties, however, has produced fuch fatal confequences, as particularly to demand the notice of Parliament.

As foon as the conftitutional change of 1782 was effected, and Ireland declared an independent nation, new grievances were ftated for redrefs, new evils were fuggefted for reform, complaints were made of inequality in the parliamentary reprefentation, and the preponderance of Englifh influence. The convention called for procuring the parliamentary reform, openly, and in the moft unqualified manner, difcuffed the plan of innovation; and to raife the political importance of this extraordinary affembly, it had its fittings in the very metropolis, attended by a confiderable guard of volunteers. The Government at length faw its danger, it remained firm, and the project of correcting and new-modelling the parliamentary reprefentation has hitherto failed.

The friends of democracy, and thofe who wifhed to eftablifh a feparate government in Ireland, finding that their own power was infufficient to attain their purpofes, and knowing that the great majority of the people of Ireland, being Catholics, and excluded from the exercife of the elective franchife, were in a great meafure indifferent to the conftitutional changes which were demanded; they therefore applied themfelves to the feduction of the Catholics, and, fufpending the open purfuit of reform and feparation from England, applied their whole force to procure a repeal of the penal laws, and the admiffion of the Catholic body to the full participation of the conftitution. The very men who were fecretly undermining the Government, and had refolved on its complete fubverfion, were obliged, in furtherance of their defigns, to declaim pub-

E   licly

licly on its excellence and the injuftice of any
portion of the King's fubjects being excluded
from the full enjoyment of fo admirable a conftitution. The former method of fpeaking to Government, through the medium of conventions
and national delegations, was again reforted to,
and again fucceeded. However, before the Catholic convention thought proper to diffolve itfelf, it voted the refolution for reform ; thus re-
quiting the fervices of their new friends by reci-
procal obligation, and concurring in hoftility to
the conftitution, into which they had been admitted.

In the year 1785, certain commercial regulations refpecting the trade of the two countries occu-
pied the attention of their refpective legiflatures.
The propofitions offered by England have been
univerfally admitted as highly promoting the intereft of Ireland. However, Great Britain confidered
it effential to the harmony of this adjuftment, and
for the further fatisfaction of both countries, that
the regulations of one fhould prevail in the other ;
that the trade and manufactures of Great Britain
and Ireland fhould enjoy the fame freedom, and
feel the fame reftraint. On this exprefs condition
was it propofed, that thofe laws which have created
and expanded the commercial power of England,
fhould be adopted occafionally in Ireland, in fimilar cafes only, and enlarging and reftraining equally in both. As this fyftem manifeftly appeared
calculated to cement the interefts of the two countries, to affimilate their commercial fyftem, to exclude the jealoufies of trade, and fully and deeply
to blend the capital, the induftry, and talents of
both, the friends of dif-union were alarmed ; they
perceived that this meafure would produce the
union which they deprecated, that it would bind
what they meant to untie : every oppofition, therefore, to the meafure was to be given. They repre-
fented

fented the conftitution of 1782 to be in danger ; the people were told that their liberty and happinefs could not furvive the ratification of this agreement. Every art which could delude a credulous, unfuf-pecting, uninveftigating nation, was practifed, and with fuccefs ; every topic of pride and felf-import-ance was urged to a people, whofe paffions, and weaknefs, and propenfities have ever been the tri-umph of its enemies. The commercial detail of the propofitions was not examined ; it was loft in their conftitutional effect. The cry of condemna-tion became general, and the meafure failed.

Since the commencement of the prefent war, England has experienced all the difficulties which are incident to the ftate of hoftility, and which re-quired the utmoft vigilance and exertion of her Government. The common enemy has been un-wearied in his aggreffions, and fingularly active and copious in his refources. He has profecuted the war by internal treachery, and fubdues nations by detaching fubjects from their government. Among the numerous objects which his principles have de-luded, and his ftratagems beguiled, Ireland is moft confpicuous and unfortunate. The enemy faw that, through her, the power of Britain might receive an irrecoverable blow, and that fhe had not only much to reward, but to folicit his attention. Her puculiar government had generated much abufe, which her imperfect connection with Eng-land had rather promoted than corrected. Great inequality of civil rights had divided her people ; and a difpofition of hoftility towards Great Britain, and for the feparation of the countries, had pro-greffively advanced. The enemy has fully availed himfelf of the ftate of Ireland and befides the ac-tivity of his ennity towards great Britain in every way in which fhe was vulnerable, his interference has been courted and invited by the difaffected in Ire-land. To refer to the particulars of the correfpon-

dence

dence between the French Government and the Societies of United Irishmen is unneceffary. The Report of the Committees of both Houfes laft feffions
is full and fatisfactory in its developement, not only
of the rebellion itfelf, but of all the preceding fteps
and machinations which led to the unhappy confequences, and prepared and organized the nation for
open violence. This Report contains a demonftration as clear as the mind of man can expect on any
fubject, that to feparate thefe courttries was the fole
ruling object of the United Societies; that all
their demands of reform and of juftice to the Catholic, were colourable only, they were pretences
to deceive the unthinking, to bribe the interefted,
and to force Government to conceffions, which by
gradual encroachment would undermine its whole
fyftem. The founder of the Society of United
Irifhmen in Dublin, the mifery of whofe laft days
fhould convey fome morality to the wicked, made it
the bafis and the firft principle of the Irifh Union,
that connexion with Britain was ruinous to Ireland.
It is this paramount object only which gives confift-
ency and uniformity of character to all the meafures
and proceedings of that execrable Society : and this
fame principle, Tone maintained on his trial, and
fealed with his death : and one of the felf-convicted
traitors, now in cuftody, had the confidence to make
the fame profeffion at the bar of Parliament, and to
enter particularly into argument that Ireland could
exift as an independent nation unconnected with
Great Britain. And it does appear by the fame parliamentary report that it was determined folemnly
by the Union not to be diverted from their great
purpofe by any conceffion of Parliament, or any
acquiefcence to their demands.

After the review which has been taken of the
hiftory of Ireland, and the particular facts which
have been adduced, the fupplement of evidence
which is furnifhed by the late rebellion, eftablifhes,
beyond

beyond all doubt, that a great degree of reftleffnefs and difquiet has long prevailed in Ireland; that her lower claffes of people have been uniformly turbulent and untractable, qualities which indifpofed them to the dominion of England, from the peaceful habits and fubordination it would produce; that religious difference and the jealoufies of property forfeited by rebellion, and transferred to Englifh fettlers, have promoted and inflamed their prejudices; and that they are ignorant, perfidious, and credulous. It appears alfo, that the American war, and the revolution in France, have produced a ftrong difpofition for change, and for new-modelling eftablifhed governments; that this fpirit has had extenfive influence in Ireland; that the American war feparated Ireland from the Englifh Legiflature; that the conduct of the Irifh Parliament in 1789 endangered the only connexion which remained, that of the executive; and that in the prefent war the dependency of Ireland on the Englifh Crown has been preferved by the force of arms only.

A feries of continual efforts anticipated the conftitutional change of 1782. From the time of the Revolution attempts had been made to eftablifh a feparate legiflature, and the embarraffment of Britain in the American war produced its accomplifhment. The King's malady and fufpenfion of the royal power produced the extraordinary decifion in 1789; and the confpiracy and rebellion in 1798 were preceded by the reception of French principles, the new enthufiafm of democracy, and by reiterated complaints againft the fyftem of corrupt influence, which after the feparation of the legiflatures remained the only poffible mode of keeping the countries together; and this confpiracy and rebellion took effect when Britain was involved in a war, the unprecedented nature of which required that fhe fhould direct her whole attention, and pour out her whole ftrength, againft the efforts of the common enemy.   Every

Every man therefore who regards the British empire is called upon to confider with ferioufnefs and attention the prefent ftate of Ireland. That there exifts within that country a confiderable body of men ftrongly difpofed to effect a difmemberment of the empire, is beyond fcepticifm to deny ; and that this difpofition is artfully concealed under pub- lic profeffions of attachment to the conftitution of England, and of claims for its full participation by reforming the parliamentary reprefentation, and giving the people more efficacy, is equally clear and indifputable. And it cannot be denied that the vices of the Irish government, its ariftocracy, and enlarged and unqualified corruption, are fufficient to give colouring to popular complaints, and to alienate the people from a connection with Eng- land, which feems to require fuch odious and mif- chievous fupports. Thefe vices can be no longer tolerated. A government which defpifes public opinion cannot long exift The public authorities fhould be refpected, and the people fhould have confidence in the legiflature. When abufes are carried to an extent which no one attempts to juf- tify, which all are ready to condemn, and which provoke fome to acts of rebellion, the public fafety is endangered, and this danger is much heightened by the extraordinary occurrences of thefe days, in which the fall of an ancient and venerable monarchy has fhaken the ftates of Europe to their foundation, and in which an infolent and prefumptuous demo- cracy affects univerfal dominion by her principles as well as arms. Ireland has confederated, and Britain is at war with this democracy. If it ftood therefore on the mere footing of policy and of felf- intereft with Great Britain, it is impoffible for her any longer to fleep over the affairs of Ireland ; fhe cannot abandon her to the enemy ; fhe cannot con- fent to her own difmemberment and difgrace. But claims of a higher nature and views, fuch as become

come Great Britain, call for her immediate interference. The late rebellion has rekindled the heat
of religious bigotry, and revived the animofities of
party. Thefe divifions in Ireland are marked with
uncommon virulence, and accompanied with peculiar atrocities. To reprefs their violence and extend the King's protection to all his Irifh fubjects,
is now a difficult exertion of his government ; but
the very moment in which the prefent vigilance is
intermitted, or that any change of government is
conceded, which fhall leffen the King's influence in
Ireland, and augment the popular power, at that
inftant the torch of civil fury will again light that
unhappy country to new fcenes of murder and de-
folation. The United Irifhmen and the whole clafs
of the difaffected are now directing their whole attention to force a Parliamentary Reform. In this
purfuit they are joined by many men of good intentions, who lament the prefent faults in the mode of
adminiftering the government of Ireland, but who
have not examined the origin of thefe faults, nor
the neceffity which has produced and continues
them, and who are equally unconfcious and unfuf-
pecting of the confequences which would infallibly
refult from the attainment of fuch a meafure. A
democratic Houfe of Commons in Ireland, and connection with England, cannot exift together ; they
are incompatible. England would foon be driven
to the deplorable neceffity of maintaining her dominion by direct and continued war, or abandoning
Ireland to the extravagance of popular afcendancy,
and the defigns of the common enemy. That an
independent Houfe of Commons would eftablifh a
republic in Ireland is as certain as any event can be
which is future, and which the mind of man can
forefee and anticipate, reafoning from what has
happened, to what may happen, from the certainty
of paft experience to the probable dependency of
like effects on like caufes in the great feries of human

man action, and feeling at the very moment of this deduction that it fhares in that great progreffion which filently, though rapidly, is accelerating the confequences it predicted.

It is not in vain that the providence of God, in fome inftances, imparts to man a portion of his intellect, to penetrate into the future, and forefee the revolutions of time. Human nature is feldom vifited by misfortune without deferving it, and knowing that it proceeds from its own omiffion or offence ; and never does God fpread before his creatures the pit of delufion and fate, without giving them facuity to fee and avoid it.

The moment has therefore come, in which the government of Great Britain is urged by its own intereft, by its parental duty towards Ireland, by the irrefiftible claims of that great portion of the Irifh people who iffued from her loins, who fhare her religious faith, and whofe property refts on Englifh title ; and, above all, by the characteriftics of the Englifh nation, her order, humanity and religion, to fave Ireland, without delay, from the evils which impend, and the deftruction to which fhe is expofed. Whatever difficulties may impede an immediate incorporation, whatever inconvenience may attend the prefent agitation of this meafure, they are as nothing to the embarraffment which will accrue, and the direful neceffity in which fhe will be involved, if the prefent occafion be neglected, and the fchemes of the difaffected prevail. Her magnanimity will encounter danger if it exift ; there will be none if fhe is firm ; fhe will regard as idle found the clamour which is raifed by the ftupid politics of fome, and the wickednefs of others ; and true to the great character of her nation, fhe will conduct herfelf with wifdom, philanthropy, and juftice.

THE END.